HAL•LEONARD
INSTRUMENTAL
PLAY-ALONG

AUDIO
ACCESS
INCLUDED

PLAYBACK+
Speed • Pitch • Balance • Loop

TENOR SAX
CHRISTMAS *Favorites*

Audio arrangements by Peter Deneff

To access audio visit:
www.halleonard.com/mylibrary
Enter Code
2542-4694-8721-7135

ISBN 978-1-4950-9636-5

7777 W. BLUEMOUND RD. P.O. BOX 13819 MILWAUKEE, WI 53213

In Australia Contact:
Hal Leonard Australia Pty. Ltd.
4 Lentara Court
Cheltenham, Victoria, 3192 Australia
Email: ausadmin@halleonard.com.au

Visit Hal Leonard Online at
www.halleonard.com

BLUE CHRISTMAS

TENOR SAX

Words and Music by BILLY HAYES
and JAY JOHNSON

THE CHRISTMAS SONG
(Chestnuts Roasting on an Open Fire)

TENOR SAX

Music and Lyric by MEL TORMÉ
and ROBERT WELLS

Slowly

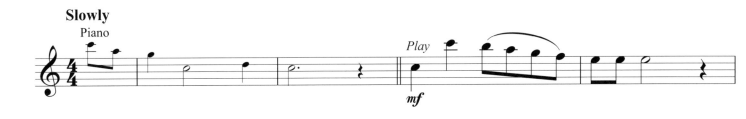

CHRISTMAS TIME IS HERE

from A CHARLIE BROWN CHRISTMAS

Words by LEE MENDELSON
Music by VINCE GUARALDI

TENOR SAX

Slowly

FELIZ NAVIDAD

TENOR SAX

Music and Lyrics by
JOSÉ FELICIANO

HAPPY XMAS
(War Is Over)

TENOR SAX

Written by JOHN LENNON
and YOKO ONO

HAVE YOURSELF A MERRY LITTLE CHRISTMAS

from MEET ME IN ST. LOUIS

TENOR SAX

Words and Music by HUGH MARTIN
and RALPH BLANE

8

HERE COMES SANTA CLAUS
(Right Down Santa Claus Lane)

TENOR SAX

Words and Music by GENE AUTRY
and OAKLEY HALDEMAN

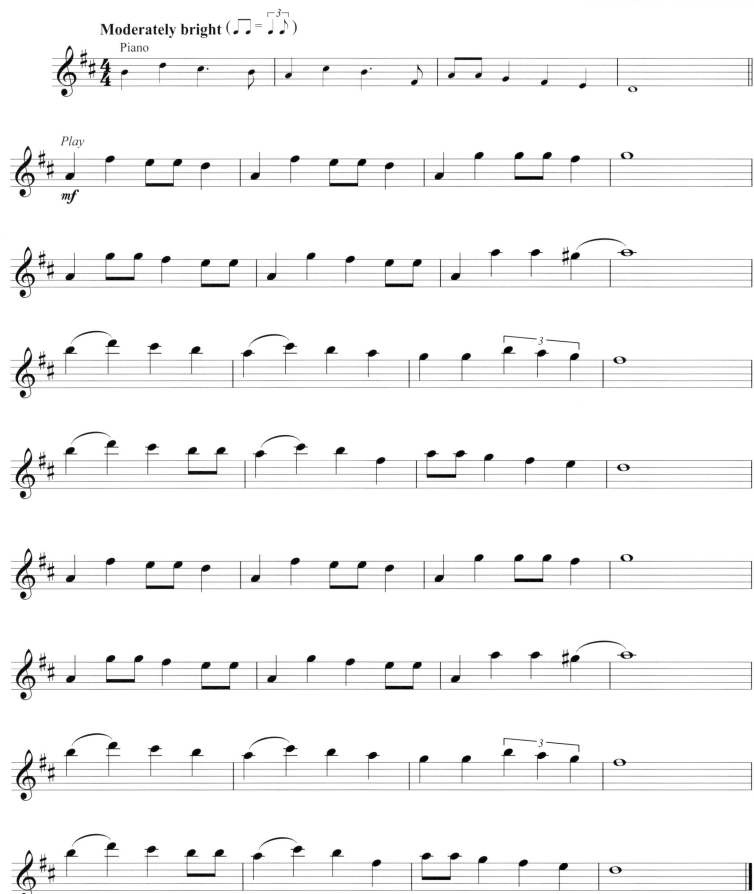

(There's No Place Like)
HOME FOR THE HOLIDAYS

TENOR SAX

Words and Music by AL STILLMAN
and ROBERT ALLEN

IT'S BEGINNING TO LOOK LIKE CHRISTMAS

TENOR SAX

By MEREDITH WILLSON

MELE KALIKIMAKA

TENOR SAX

Words and Music by
R. ALEX ANDERSON

MERRY CHRISTMAS, DARLING

TENOR SAX

Words and Music by RICHARD CARPENTER
and FRANK POOLER

ROCKIN' AROUND THE CHRISTMAS TREE

TENOR SAX

Music and Lyrics by
JOHNNY MARKS

RUDOLPH THE RED-NOSED REINDEER

TENOR SAX

Music and Lyrics by
JOHNNY MARKS

SILVER AND GOLD

TENOR SAX

Music and Lyrics by
JOHNNY MARKS